The Secret Garden of ~ GEORGE ~ WASHINGTON CARVER

Written by Gene Barretta   Illustrated by Frank Morrison

KT KATHERINE TEGEN BOOKS
An Imprint of HarperCollins Publishers

Library of Congress Control Number: 2018958892
ISBN 978-0-06-243015-1 (trade bdg.) — ISBN 978-0-06-243018-2 (pbk.)

The artist used oil on illustration board to create the illustrations for this book.
Typography by Rachel Zegar
22 23 24 25 26   RTLO   19 18 17 16 15 14 13 12 11 10

First Edition

For Nanie & Grandad, and Grandmom
& Grandpop. Strong roots in my garden.
A special thank-you to Curtis Gregory,
Ben Goldberg, and Ben Barretta.
—G.B.

To the genius in my house, my son, Nasir
—F.M.

WASHINGTON, DC, 1921
GEORGE WASHINGTON CARVER
ADDRESSES THE US CONGRESS.

"We are just beginning to learn the value of the peanut," Carver told the congressmen. Some of them laughed. One man made a racist remark. As a Black man speaking to a room of all-white representatives, Carver was not among friends.

African Americans were still segregated by US federal law and treated as second-class citizens.

Carver had been given only ten minutes to speak. He gave the audience ten minutes they would never forget.

Carver showed them how peanuts could be used to make dozens of items, including face cream, soaps, ink, cheese, instant coffee, paper, paints, glue, and much more. When his time was up, they were impressed. The chairman encouraged him to continue. "Go ahead, brother, your time is unlimited." Carver spoke for over an hour.

From the time he was a boy, he had a deep desire to share what he knew.
So then, why did he once have a secret garden?

DIAMOND GROVE, MISSOURI, 1874

No one knew about the garden George kept hidden on the Carver farm. No one saw how the child cared for his flowers and how much he loved them.

When he watered the clovers, their petals curved up like a smile. The black-eyed Susans winked when he patted the soil around their roots. He sang to the dandelions, and they waved to him with their long leaves.

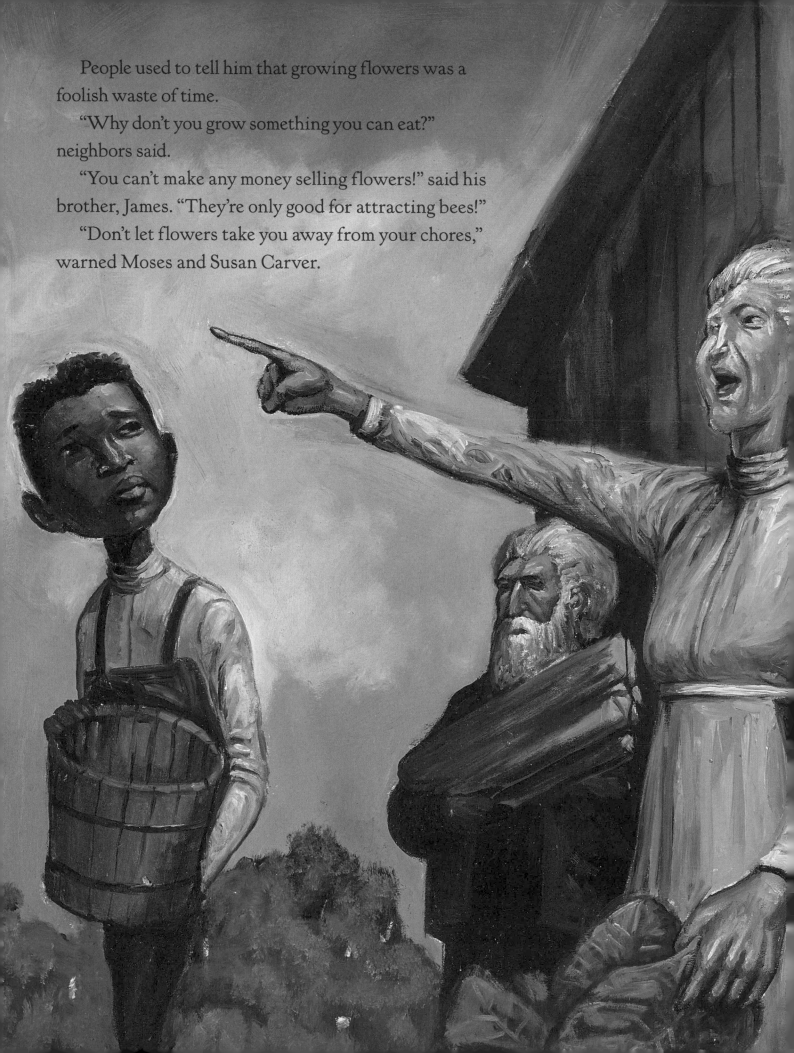

People used to tell him that growing flowers was a foolish waste of time.

"Why don't you grow something you can eat?" neighbors said.

"You can't make any money selling flowers!" said his brother, James. "They're only good for attracting bees!"

"Don't let flowers take you away from your chores," warned Moses and Susan Carver.

George was born in 1864. Like his mother and his brother, he was enslaved on the Carver farm. While still a baby, George and his mother were kidnapped. Days later, he was found close to death and brought back to the Carvers. His mother was never seen again. The next year, slavery was outlawed in the United States.

Moses and Susan Carver did not have children of their own and raised George and his brother on the farm. George was a sickly child, which meant less time working and more time exploring. He filled the house with a steady stream of interesting plants and rocks.

Susan taught him how to be creative with the little they had. Nothing was wasted.

Turkey feathers were used to make sewing needles.

They made dyes from nuts and berries.

They used plants and leaves for medicine.

Every day, he ran into the woods to discover something new. "I want to know the name of every stone and flower and insect and bird and beast," he said.

Education was limited at home. George had only one book, which he read dozens of times. "I know this book by heart," he told Susan. "I wish I could go to school with the white children."

Slavery had ended, but US segregation laws still denied Black people the same rights as whites. George decided to create his own classroom in the woods and studied the subject he loved most—nature. And no matter how much people discouraged him, he wanted to grow flowers.

George decided to grow them in a secret garden so no one could find them or tease him.

It became a magical place for him. Tiny seeds went into the dirt and transformed into beautiful flowers. In his mind, the garden was a true gift from God, whom he called the Great Creator.

Each day, George rolled the soil between his fingers to make sure it wasn't too wet or too dry. Some plants needed more rain and some needed more sun.

"Come here. You need a haircut," George said as he cradled a daisy in his hand and clipped off its dry petals. He spread them around the soil to help the flowers grow.

At first, the gardening was difficult because he couldn't ask for help and reveal his secret. The more he experimented, the more he learned.

George studied each new season by painting the life
cycles of the flowers. Berries were used to make paints.
Twigs and grass were used to make brushes.

He learned how to protect the roots through the winter so flowers could be reborn in the spring. "Welcome back," he whispered to the tiny sprouts.

It was a special garden and could have remained secret forever. But, eventually, the young boy's generosity changed that.

When George met a neighbor with a sick plant or flower, he offered to care for it. Part of his garden became a plant hospital. Wilting plants went in and blooming plants came out.

No one could believe that such a small child had so many big ideas. "Here comes the Plant Doctor," they'd say whenever he paid a visit.

"Think of all the people I can help," he told the garden. It inspired him to see their flowers growing side by side with his flowers. George breathed a sigh of relief. "There's no need to be secret anymore."

George knew there was much to see and learn away from the farm. At the age of twelve, he said goodbye to his garden and set off on his own for a new adventure.

In Neosho, Missouri, he lived with Mariah Watkins, who gave him advice he carried into adulthood: "Learn all you can, George. Then give it all back to our people."

Over the next eighteen years, he lived in several states and attended many schools to study art and agriculture.

It was not easy. After being accepted to Highland College in 1885, the all-white school refused to admit him when they learned he was African American.

But the young man was determined to get an education. In 1896, George Washington Carver became the first Black man to study at, graduate from, and teach at Iowa Agricultural College.

The same year, Booker T. Washington, president of the Tuskegee Institute, hired him to teach agriculture. When Carver first arrived, he said, "Everything looked hungry. The land, the cotton, the cattle, the people." Farmers were in trouble. Cotton crops were destroying their land. With little money and second-rate equipment, Carver built Tuskegee's first farming laboratory.

He experimented with new crops to replace cotton, like sweet potatoes and soybeans. But the peanut was his champion. It had nutrients to nourish and refresh the soil. He convinced farmers to grow peanuts and then developed over three hundred uses for them. It wasn't long before peanuts became the largest crop in the South.

Carver also created a traveling schoolhouse called the Jesup Agricultural Wagon to visit poor farmers. It offered everything from tool demonstrations to medical care to pamphlets on how to improve farms and live healthier. In its first summer, the wagon visited over six thousand people.

Carver's advice saved countless farms and families. "What would you like to learn today?" he asked a farmer. "The best time to plow or how to raise a strong cow?"

Wherever he traveled, people went to hear him speak. After his historic day in front of the US Congress, he became a living folk hero. He was also recognized as an early environmentalist, a voice for racial harmony, and an adviser to world leaders. With his new fame came many awards and honors. Yet he remained a humble man, always ready to serve humanity.

Since his days on the Carver farm, one thing never changed.
"Day after day I spent in the woods alone, in order to collect my floral beauties, and put them in my little garden I had hidden in the brush not far from the house."

"It has always been the one ideal of my life
to be of the greatest good to the greatest
number of my people possible."

Timeline

1864
- George is born into slavery on the Carver farm in Diamond Grove, Missouri. To this day, no one knows his exact birth date.
- His father, Giles, dies in an ox cart accident before George is born.
- His mother, Mary, and George are kidnapped and taken across state lines to be sold. George is rescued. His mother is never seen again.

1865
- The Thirteenth Amendment to the US Constitution is passed, outlawing slavery in the United States.

1867
- As a child, George is often sick with whooping cough and croup. Doctors say he will not live past the age of twenty-one.

1876
- George is prevented from attending school because of Jim Crow segregation laws in the South that did not grant the same rights to African Americans as white people. So he moves to Neosho, Missouri, to attend the Neosho Colored School. He lives with Andrew and Mariah Watkins. George chooses an official last name, Carver.

1878
- He moves to Fort Scott, Kansas, looking for a better education. He leaves that town after he witnesses a Black man getting killed on the street.

1879
- He moves to Olathe, Kansas, to attend school. He lives with Ben and Lucy Seymour and helps with their laundry business. A year later, he moves with them to Minneapolis, Kansas.

1883
- George visits the Carver farm and discovers that his brother, James, has died from smallpox.

1885
- George graduates from high school in Minneapolis, Kansas.
- George adopts the middle name "Washington" to avoid confusion with another George Carver.
- He is accepted to Highland College in

Kansas. When he arrives, he is turned away because of his skin color.

1890

- George is the first Black student to enroll at Simpson College in Iowa. He studies art.

1891

- His teacher at Simpson recognizes his interest in plants and convinces him to transfer to Iowa Agricultural College.

1896

- George Washington Carver is the first Black man to graduate from Iowa Agricultural College with a master's degree.
- Booker T. Washington, the president of the Tuskegee Institute in Alabama, hires Carver to develop their agricultural department.
- The same year, the Supreme Court makes segregation legal throughout the United States with the *Plessy v. Ferguson* decision.

1906

- Carver develops a traveling schoolhouse called the Jesup Agricultural Wagon to educate local farmers.

1916

- British scientists make him a fellow at the English Royal Society for the Encouragement of the Arts.

1921

- Carver addresses the US Congress (the House of Representatives Ways & Means Committee).

1923

- The NAACP awards him the Spingarn Medal for outstanding achievement.

1928

- Carver receives an honorary doctorate of science from Simpson College.

1939

- Carver is awarded an honorary membership from the American Inventors Society.

1940

- Carver establishes the George Washington Carver Foundation.

1943

- George Washington Carver dies on January 5, 1943. He never married or had children.
- The George Washington Carver National Monument is established at his birthplace in Missouri.

1945

- The US Congress designates January 5 (the anniversary of his death) as George Washington Carver Recognition Day.

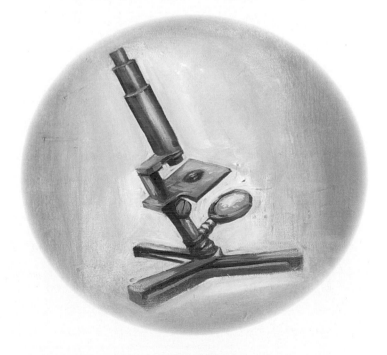

Bibliography

Kremer, Gary R., ed. *George Washington Carver: In His Own Words*. Columbia, MO:
    University of Missouri Press, 1991.

Modern Marvels. "George Washington Carver Tech." History Channel, 2005.

Vella, Christina. *George Washington Carver: A Life*. Baton Rouge, LA: LSU Press, 2015.

Further Reading

Bolden, Tonya. *George Washington Carver*. New York: Abrams Books for Young Readers, 2015.

Gigliotti, Jim. *Who Was George Washington Carver?* New York: Grosset & Dunlap, 2015.

Harness, Cheryl. *The Groundbreaking, Chance-Taking Life of George Washington Carver and
    Science & Invention in America*. Washington, DC: National Geographic, 2008.

Nelson, Marilyn. *Carver: A Life in Poems*. Asheville, NC: Front Street, 2001.